KINGDOM ✝ PROMISES
Evotions Empowered by Biblical Statements of Faith

WE ARE

KEN HEMPHILL

B&H
PUBLISHING GROUP

NASHVILLE, TENNESSEE

KINGDOM PROMISES: **WE ARE**

ISBN 0-8054-2781-3

B&H Publishing Group
Nashville, Tennessee
www.BHPublishingGroup.com

Dewey Decimal Classification: 242.5
Devotional Literature / Faith
Printed in the United States
4 5 6 7   12 11 10 09

PREFACE

Studying God's Word always brings its own rewards. I have been deeply moved by the study of these simple statements that are scattered throughout the Word of God. It is my prayer that they will minister in your life as they have mine. I thank you for your willingness to buy this book and allow me to be your guide as the Holy Spirit informs your mind and transforms your heart.

As always, I am indebted to my wife, who is my partner in ministry and my encourager in this ministry of writing. She brings the order and solitude to our home that makes it possible for me to reflect and write. She is often the source of ideas that soon appear in my books. Our devotional times together frequently become theological discussions which enrich my understanding.

My children are a constant joy to me, and our growing family provides a rich context for writing. Tina and Brett have been blessed with a daughter, Lois, who is as active as her "papa." Rachael and Trey

It is an honor to dedicate this book
to my sister and brother-in-law:

{ Dot and Bill Helms }

Dot is the big sister who
instilled in me a passion for learning.
She and Bill have modeled who
"We Are" in Christ through caring
for Mom and Dad during
their declining years.

were blessed with a daughter, Emerson, whose smile lights up a room. It is a joy to watch Katie and Daniel grow in marital love and in the Lord. My family is the context for my entire ministry.

I want to thank Morris Chapman, the visionary leader of the Southern Baptist Convention for calling our denomination to focus on God's Kingdom. He has given me the freedom to write those things God lays on my heart. All of my colleagues at the Executive Committee of the Southern Baptist Convention have encouraged me in this new phase of ministry.

As usual the good folks at Broadman and Holman have been my partners in this ministry. I am challenged by the trust they place in me. Ken Stephens has led Broadman and Holman with integrity of heart. I can't begin to express my gratitude to Lawrence Kimbrough, my partner in this writing adventure. Lawrence is far more than an editor. He is a friend, colleague, and artist. What he does with a rough draft is a thing of beauty.

This book is somewhat of a new genre. It looks like a daily devotional in its format, but it is written to be "bite-sized" theology. I have attempted to explain each of these great Kingdom Promises in its original context and then to apply it to life. Thus, I highly recommend that you read this book with your Bible open, because the focal passages will have the greatest impact on you as you see them in context. You might also want to consider using these verses as a Scripture memory project while you're reading.

I pray God will use His Word to bring encouragement to your heart. And if this book of Kingdom Promises speaks life to you and ministers to your needs, I hope you'll pass it along to someone else.

Ken Hemphill
Nashville, Tennessee
Spring 2006

Foreword

This brief book is designed to assist the reader to experience spiritual kingdom growth in order to represent Christ with strength and purpose throughout any geographical or social setting.

Often Dr. Hemphill uses illustrations directly out of his own life, which add warmth and spiritual depth to his biblical interpretations. For instance, his reflections on the love of his parents when he was afraid of the dark as a young child, on the pleasure of playing football even for a coach who would not give the team time for a water break, on growing up near a Baptist children's home, and on the aroma of food being cooked on a wood stove at his grandmother's house make for enjoyable reading.

I gained new spiritual insights from reading *Kingdom Promises: We Are.* I predict that everyone who reads the book will reach the same conclusion.

Dr. Carlisle Driggers, Executive Director
South Carolina Baptist Convention

WE ARE
the Salt of the Earth

I played high school football in the
days before a water break was mandatory.
In fact, if the issue had been left up to our
coach, the sport would never have become
enlightened to the need for players to
replenish fluids. He was a strict disciplinar-
ian who thought that wearing your helmet
throughout practice and going without
water made men out of boys.

Before my senior year, however, the
rule came down requiring coaches to give
water breaks to their players. It was also
about this time that we discovered the
value of salt tablets in regulating the chemi-
cal balance of the body and prohibiting the
cramping of muscles. So our coach came
up with a way to combine these two while
still accomplishing his old-school purposes:
he dumped salt into our drinking water.

Needless to say, the water break didn't
cure our thirst. Instead, it had the opposite

effect. The salt in the water just made us thirstier.

As Christians, we need to recognize that we are designed to *create thirst*. Just as peanuts and popcorn beg to be eaten with a cold soft drink or a refreshing lemonade, we should seek to make others thirsty for Christ through our pure, flavorful lives. Otherwise, we're like salt which has become tasteless, flavorless, useless, "no longer good for anything but to be thrown out and trampled on by men" (v. 13).

It was common in Palestine to see mounds of worthless salt scattered in piles on the ground, much the same way as crushed seashells line the walkway at a beach. That's because when the usefulness had seeped out of the salt crystals, dissolving them to a tasteless enough level, no one had any need for it. Salt-less salt is absurd, but no more so than Christianity that has lost its taste and attractiveness. Believers in Christ are not designed to blend in blandly with society but to bring seasoning and life, to add a noticeable difference to ordinary living, to deliver a punch and purity that causes others to thirst for righteousness.

WE ARE
the Light of the World

> **Matthew 5:14** You are the light of the world. A city situated on a hill cannot be hidden.

Because I was the youngest in my family, I went to bed earlier than anyone else in the house. I remember often lying there alone in the dark while the outside light, the wind, and the weeping willow tree in our backyard combined to create the most unusual shapes on my wall. Some of the shadows seemed to take on a life of their own. As my fear mounted, I would cry out to Mom and Dad. But as soon as they opened the door and turned on the light, the shadows would recede and my fears would dissipate.

Yes, light has a way of changing our environment.

When we become followers of Jesus, we are called to be light. Paul stated it this way: "Do everything without grumbling and arguing, so that you may be blameless and pure, children of God who are faultless in a crooked and perverted generation, among whom you shine like stars in the world" (Phil. 2:14–15). Both our behavior ("blameless and pure") and our attitude ("without grumbling and arguing") should set us apart from unbelievers.

But for light to have an impact, it must be made visible. That's why Jesus commanded us not to place our light "under a basket" but to position ourselves like "a city situated on a hill" (vv. 14–15) — not in order to draw attention to ourselves but to illuminate Another. We may sometimes feel shy about attracting this kind of notice, but our light is actually a reflection of the light of *Christ*, who lives inside us.

Jesus came to bring illumination into a world made dark by sin, shining so brightly that the crowds wanted to listen and follow him. He made it clear that when people looked upon him, they were seeing the Father (John 14:9).

So like him, our desire is that those who see our good works will "give glory to [our] Father in heaven" (v. 16). Christians are to live in such a distinctive manner that the light which beams from our lives will draw and direct people to God.

WE ARE
Witnesses of the Gospel

> **Luke 24:48** You are
> witnesses of these things.

I grew up in the era of Perry Mason, the famous TV lawyer. I watched each week with eager anticipation as he called witness after witness to the stand. He would question them concerning what they had seen, building his case based on the coherence and integrity of the story told by these credible witnesses. Their testimony always formed the heart of his argument.

Jesus told his early followers that they were "witnesses" of his life, death, and resurrection. He had "opened their minds" so they could understand the way he fulfilled all that had been written about him in the "Law of Moses, the Prophets, and the Psalms" (vv. 44–45). As such, these eyewitnesses were given the unique opportunity and responsibility of heralding the good news to all nations, announcing to them that redemption was now available through the resurrected Christ.

I know what you may be thinking: *I'm not an apostle and I'm not an eyewitness.* Technically, I know, that's true—but not completely. Because when we come to a personal knowledge of Christ, we too become *eyewitnesses* to his grace in our own lives. No one else can tell the story of our experience with Christ the way we can.

We are also *apostles* in a sense—a word that means "sent one." The apostle Paul made it clear that once we received reconciliation with God through Christ, we became responsible for sharing this news with others. We are "ambassadors for Christ" (2 Cor. 5:20), commissioned to take the good news to the world. This is both a responsibility and a privilege.

Yes, being a witness is a high calling, requiring deliberate effort. But I have good news for you. Just as Jesus promised his first followers to wait for the presence and power of the Holy Spirit (v. 49), you, too, do not have to accomplish this task in your own strength. In fact, you *can't* do it in your strength. But the Holy Spirit will empower you to be his witness.

WE ARE
the Branches in God's Vine

{
John 15:5 I am the vine;
you are the branches.
}

We should not overlook the intimacy
of this familiar image from Scripture. The
connection between the vine and the
branches is so close that the branch actually *abides* in the vine. Equally amazing is
the fact that the vine and its indwelling
branches are superintended by the Father
himself, the "vineyard keeper" (v. 1). Our
Father loves us so much—imagine this!—
he personally oversees the condition of
our life with Christ.

This is why the vine-and-branches
imagery only holds true for those who have
experienced a personal relationship with
Jesus, who have been grafted in through
faith in Christ and are enabled by God's
grace to remain attached to the vine.

Everything the Father does to and for
the branches is designed to enable us to
bear much fruit—a fruit which should
grow naturally through our attachment

to the vine, a fruit which should mirror the kinds of actions and characteristics Jesus displayed during his earthly life. When we bear spiritual fruit, we "prove" ourselves to be his disciples and we glorify the Father (v. 8). Truly, the branch can do "nothing" apart from Christ (v. 5).

But the idea that we can do nothing without Christ is something we find hard to accept. We like to believe we can at least do *some* things apart from him, that we only need to rely on him when we encounter difficult challenges. The Christian life, however, is one that is wholly dependent on the life that flows through the vine.

Once we have been grafted in, it is our responsibility as branches to "remain" in the vine, which requires radical obedience to the Word (v. 10). The Father helps us do this by pruning us to ensure our fruitfulness. This requires him to cut sinful activities from our lives and remove those things that distract us from having a singular focus on Christ. We can be assured, though, that his actions are always loving, not intended to harm or damage us but directed at enabling us to bear fruit.

WE ARE
Friends of Jesus

> **John 15:14** You are My friends if you do what I command you.

There is a certain bond between close friends. We can be apart for an extended period of time, but when we meet again it's as if we were together yesterday. With true friends we can share our secret pains and our greatest aspirations.

But friendship also implies responsibility. Thus it is not surprising for Jesus to indicate that his friends obey his commands. As friends of Christ, we know that his word to us is always reliable, and therefore our desire is to obey.

Along with the *responsibilities* of friendship with Christ, however, there are also *privileges*. Listen to verse 15: "I do not call you slaves anymore, because a slave doesn't know what his master is doing. I have called you friends, because I have made known to you everything I have heard from My Father." Jesus opened his heart to his disciples, sharing with them all that the Father had disclosed to him. He didn't treat them like slaves; he embraced them as friends. He held nothing back.

We don't have the privilege of face-to-face friendship with Jesus the way the first-century disciples did, but we are still included in this "we are" promise. Jesus laid down his life for us just as he did for *them* (v. 13). We have his teaching in written form, and we possess the Holy Spirit who enables us to understand and obey his Word (v. 26).

This is one of my favorite "we are" passages, because it teaches that Jesus has *chosen* us to be his friends (v. 16) — not because of any merit on our part, but at the high price of his sovereign love. Such grace is hard to comprehend!

Are you spending sufficient time with your Friend to know his heart? Are you sharing your deepest pains and your greatest joys with him? Have you told anyone else about your best friend, Jesus? Have you talked with him today yourself? It doesn't require a long-distance call to contact him. Whisper a prayer. He hears and he will answer you.

WE ARE
Called by Christ

> **Romans 1:6** We have received grace . . . including yourselves who are also Jesus Christ's by calling.

In Christian circles we sometimes use the term *calling* to refer to a person's vocation, his life's work. We speak of a missionary or a pastor as being "called" to their particular ministries. In Romans 1:1, for example, Paul referred to his own unique call to be an apostle—"singled out" for his position as a proclaimer of "God's good news."

But while it is true that certain individuals do have a unique ministry calling, it is equally true that *all* Christians are "Jesus Christ's by calling." That's what Paul was saying in verse 6 to the Christians living in Rome during the first century. And by extension he was saying this about all of us. Translated literally, this text says we are "called to be Jesus Christ's," that we are his property. We belong to him. We stand in a unique relationship with the Son because of the Father's divine call.

Can you believe God loves you so much that he called you to be his own? Can you fathom a love so deep that he purchased you for himself at the price of his own Son? Can you come to grips with the fact that he created you with absolute worth and chose you for his own purpose? This is hard to believe for all of us.

For some, however, it's even harder. Perhaps you are one who struggles with low self-esteem. You don't attribute much worth to the things you do or the person you are. You have a poor self-image and don't think you're very special. You see yourself as less than ordinary. Perhaps you haven't accomplished many of the goals and dreams you had set for yourself, or you haven't received a great deal of affirmation from the significant people in your life.

Then let this be the verse the Holy Spirit uses to remind you just how loved and cherished you are by your heavenly Father. You belong to the King by divine call. You are "Jesus Christ's by calling." Doesn't this add some purpose to the things you'll be doing today?

WE ARE
the Saints of God

Saints is one of the most commonly
used terms in the New Testament to refer
to Christians. It is generally used in its
plural form, referring back to the people
of God in the Old Testament.

This doesn't mean that we saints are
perfect, of course. It does mean, however,
that we are separated from the world, that
we are bound to Jesus Christ. Not only did
God call us, he also set us apart for himself.

Sometimes an artist will indicate that
one of his paintings is "not for sale." The
artist possesses a special affection for the
painting and has marked it as one he wants
to keep. God, the great Artist of mankind,
has likewise labeled you with a "not for
sale" sign and has set you apart for himself.

But as with everything, privilege comes
with responsibility. Being separated unto
Christ ultimately means we must separate
ourselves from the things of the world. The

knowledge that we are saints of God should have a profound impact on the things we do, the places we go, and the things we watch. Our behavior, language, and attitude should always reflect the nature of the One to whom we belong. Belonging to him has moral consequences. Thus to be a saint also means that we should desire to live a holy life.

As Christians, we are called by God to be holy people. This affirms that he desires to use us for his purposes, and that we are to keep ourselves available for his use.

Perhaps it's hard for you to imagine that the sovereign God of the universe desires to work through you. Then I have some really great news for you. In Romans 8:27, Paul gave us this incredible reminder: "He who searches the hearts knows the Spirit's mind-set, because He intercedes for the saints according to the will of God." Therefore, because we have been "called as saints," we can be assured that the Spirit is praying for us. There is nothing we will face today that we can't handle as one of God's saints.

WE ARE
Justified before God

{ **Romans 3:24** They are justified freely by His grace through the redemption that is in Christ Jesus. }

No word is more characteristic of Paul's vocabulary than *justified*. It means to "make right" or "to clear." In practical terms, it means we are acquitted in God's court. Notice, too, that this justification is given "freely" to us. This is vitally important to remember. We are justified as a gift, not by our own merit. There is nothing we can do to atone for our own sin.

To most Jews of Paul's day, this idea was truly groundbreaking. Not having knowledge of God's grace, they hoped that through observing the law they might be pronounced righteous by a holy God. Yet Paul declared in the words of the psalmist, "There is no one righteous, not even one" (v. 10). The difficulty with any attempt on our part to achieve righteousness through an accumulation of good works is this: we can never be truly convinced we have made the grade.

But now—in Christ—the whole process is reversed. God pronounces us "justified" as a gift of his grace, based not on our works but upon Christ's work on our behalf. This incredible truth has caused many Bible teachers to comment that justification means this: God looks at me "just as if I'd never sinned."

You may be asking how this is possible. The answer is found in the last phrase of this verse: "through the redemption that is in Christ Jesus." When Jesus died on the cross, he died for our sin. His death paid the price of our sin, making it possible for us to be "justified." And according to verse 22, this justification is available "to all who believe." When any of us admit our inability to resolve our sin problem, when we turn by faith to Jesus Christ, we can receive God's redemption made possible through his Son.

Isn't it a wonderful truth to know we are justified? If you have never made this wonderful discovery, why not ask Christ to forgive your sin and to be your personal Lord and Savior? If you have, tell someone about this free gift today.

WE ARE
Walking in Newness of Life

> **Romans 6:4** Just as Christ was raised from the dead . . . we too may walk in a new way of life.

The image of *walking* is an important one in the New Testament. You're certainly familiar, for example, with the concept of "walking in the Spirit"—conducting your life under his guidance and control, enjoying his continual direction and empowerment. In our present passage we find the incredible truth that we are able as believers to walk "in a new way of life." This ability to live in daily freshness is based on the fact that we have died to sin, so that we no longer have to say "yes" to it.

Before we became Christians, we were often powerless to say "no" to the passions that led us away from God. All of us can identify even now with the struggle we go through to control our anger or passion by inner fortitude alone. We frequently lose this battle for a very basic reason: when we won't submit to Christ, we are slaves of sin. But it doesn't have to be this way.

Our salvation experience was made possible by Jesus' death and resurrection—a reality depicted in the act of baptism. In the New Testament era, baptism followed immediately upon one's confession of faith. This was generally a public event where the individual was completely immersed in water. Going down into the water symbolized death, and coming up out of the water symbolized resurrection. Thus it portrays our participation with Christ. Through him we are able to walk daily in his resurrection life.

This resurrection life is not something waiting for us in the future, unavailable until after this life is over. It is a present reality. We are new creatures, empowered to live a life that is pleasing to God—right now, in this hour.

Therefore, we must commit ourselves daily to live according to our new nature which has been given to us by Christ, and to refuse to obey our old nature. When we are tempted to sin, we can declare that we are walking in newness of life—a new way of living that no longer has any need for sin and its harmful side-effects.

WE ARE
in the Spirit

> **Romans 8:9** You, however, are not in the flesh, but in the Spirit, since the Spirit of God lives in you.

Paul introduced this "we are" statement by contrasting it against its negative counterpart. Yes, we are "in the Spirit," but we "are not in the flesh." That's good to know, since Paul declared in verse 8 that those who *are* in the flesh—those who are devoid of the Spirit—"are unable to please God."

Only the Spirit of God can bring us into a living relationship with Christ. Thus if one does not have the Spirit, he does not belong to Christ.

I occasionally hear people speak as if we can separate the experience of the new birth from that of receiving the Spirit. A Christian may be asked by a well-meaning friend, "Do you have the Spirit?" This person implies that we receive the Spirit subsequent to our salvation. But we cannot belong to Christ *at all* until we are "in the Spirit."

This is why another way to speak of the Spirit's indwelling presence is to say that "Christ is in you" (v. 10). When Christ's Spirit dwells in you, your physical body is still subject to temporal death, but the Spirit that has taken up residence in you gives you eternal life.

Many people fear death. They assume this life is all there is. Others live in the vain hope that they will get another chance at life through reincarnation. But those who are in the Spirit need not worry about what happens after physical death, for we are assured the Spirit of him "who raised Christ from the dead" lives in us (v. 11).

This life-giving Spirit also empowers us to put to death the "deeds of the body" (v. 13), allowing us to live a victorious Christian life. What specific areas of the flesh cause you the greatest struggle? Do you find yourself defeated by envy, jealousy, impure thoughts, greed, or anger? You don't have to be defeated in any of these areas any longer, because you are "in the Spirit," who continuously and progressively gives you the power to resist evil and live for God.

WE ARE
Sons of God

I grew up in Thomasville, North
Carolina, the site of Mills Home Orphan-
age. This Southern Baptist-operated
children's home had an idyllic campus.
Some of my best friends in school were
young men who lived there. My parents
would frequently invite one of them to
spend the weekend with us, and we would
always treat our guest just like a member
of the family.

Sometimes, as we would drive one of
the boys back to the Mills Home campus
on Sunday afternoon, I would feel a little
bit of jealousy. My eyes danced across the
ball fields, all the way to the Olympic-sized
swimming pool. When we arrived at the
cottage of my orphan friend, we would be
greeted by a yard full of boys our same age.
I thought this was about as close to heaven
as a child could ever want to be. But when
I once expressed this jealous thought of

mine to one of my orphan friends, he quickly replied that he would gladly trade it all for one thing. "For what?" I asked.

"A dad who loves me."

We do indeed have a heavenly Father who loves us—a distinctive privilege of sonship which Paul immediately contrasted in verse 15 with the "spirit of slavery." Slavery (then as now) always leads to bondage and fear. Sonship, however, enables us to address God intimately and personally. As believers, we are privileged to call God by the same name Jesus used. That's why it is not insignificant that Jesus taught his disciples to pray to "our Father." As children of God, we have been given the privilege of intimate daily access to the Father. We are chosen by him, given his name, made heirs to his estate, and promised daily access to his presence and counsel.

Since we are children of the King, why do we often live as slaves to sin? Why don't we take full advantage of the privileges of sonship? Why do we spend so little time with him? If you are his child, determine today to live according to your heritage.

WE ARE
More than Conquerors

> **Romans 8:37** In all these things we are more than victorious through Him who loved us.

The Nike swoosh has become one of the most recognizable logos in the sports industry. The word *nike* comes from a Greek word that means "conqueror." Interestingly, the word translated "more than victorious" or "overwhelmingly conquer" in verse 37 is *hupernikomen* in the Greek. In other words, we are "super-nikes." Super-conquerors!

By the way, this verb which I translate "super-conquerors" is actually in the present tense, which even intensifies the idea. It means that we *keep* on being super-conquerors! This is the present and daily reality of our lives as Christians.

To fully comprehend the depth of this promise, it is helpful to read verses 31–37 together, where Paul asked four pointed questions: "Who is against us?" (v. 31), "Who can bring an accusation against God's elect?" (v. 33), "Who is the one who condemns?" (v. 34), and "Who can separate us from the love of Christ?" (v. 35). The victorious answer to each question is a resounding "no one" and "nothing!" As Paul wrote in verse 31, "If God is for us, who is against us?"

The fact that God would take the radical step of giving his Son to pay the penalty for our redemption—while we were still sinners!—should assure us that nothing can separate us from him or his promises. We can rest assured today that no pressure, circumstance, or unseen evil force can separate us from the love of God. These biblical truths should make us feel totally secure.

Therefore, I would highly recommend that you memorize verses 37–39 and quote them to yourself regularly. "In all these things we are more than victorious through Him who loved us. For I am persuaded that neither death nor life, nor angels nor rulers, nor things present, nor things to come, nor powers, nor height, nor depth, nor any other created thing will have the power to separate us from the love of God that is in Christ Jesus our Lord!"

WE ARE
One Body

> **Romans 12:5** We who are many are one body in Christ and individually members of one another.

The title of this book, *We Are,* (as opposed to *I Am*) was not only taken from Scripture but was intentionally chosen to illustrate the corporate nature of our Christian faith. The Bible knows nothing of "lone ranger" Christianity. Yet today our emphasis on rugged individualism and personal freedom threatens to undermine the corporate aspects of our faith.

I frequently encounter people who claim to be Christians and yet argue that they have no need or desire for fellowship with other believers. They claim they can worship quite adequately on the bank of a river or on the local golf course. They argue that their faith is solely a private matter. While it is true that each individual must personally accept Christ as Savior and be born again, it is equally true that we are born into a family. This is precisely what Paul meant when he declared that "we who are many are one body in Christ." The comparison of the Christian community to a human body illustrates the corporate nature of our faith and describes how we work together despite our diversity.

But Paul took the illustration a step further when he declared that we are "individually members of one another." This means that all Christians are interrelated and interdependent. This diversity is necessary for the body to work together effectively, but it also demands that we have unity of mind and purpose. It requires us to acknowledge that we need each other if we are to become all that God desires. As Paul wrote, the members of the body should have "concern for each other." And when "one member suffers" or when "one member is honored," the rest of us should be impacted by it (1 Cor. 12:25–26).

Have you found your place in Christ's body of believers, the church? God has designed you with purpose, redeemed you by his grace, and chosen you to be a productive part of Christ's body here on earth. You will never be complete until you are properly related to others in his family.

WE ARE
Strong for the Weak

> **Romans 15:1** We who are strong have an obligation to bear the weaknesses of those without strength.

You may not be feeling particularly strong today spiritually, but I promise you this: God's Word affirms that you are. (We will actually look at this "we are" statement two more times — in 2 Corinthians 12:10 and 1 John 2:14. Each passage underlines the same truth but makes a slightly different application.)

This "we are" promise is a humbling truth, because we know this strength is not our own. It is a gift of God. The resources to live the Christian life abundantly are made available to us only by the indwelling presence of the Holy Spirit.

But furthermore, reading this "we are" affirmation within the context of Romans 15 teaches us an additional part of its truth: with strength comes responsibility. When we as children were assigned the task of caring for a younger brother or sister, our parents reminded us that we possessed the strength and maturity to care for a weaker sibling. Paul made virtually the same application in this passage, teaching us that we must bear the weaknesses of others "and not to please ourselves" (v. 1).

We must therefore go beyond merely *tolerating* their weaknesses. We must assist them as they struggle under their loads—not in order to exhibit our greater strength, but simply because we are family and we care for one another. Christians cannot live self-centered lives. We must always be God-centered and others-focused.

As Paul wrote in verse 2, "Each one of us must please his neighbor for his good, in order to build him up." That's a radical way of living, diametrically opposed to the "looking out for number one" credo many people live by. But being strong for others is the lifestyle modeled by Christ—"for even the Messiah did not please Himself" (v. 3)—and it requires supernatural strength. So even when you don't feel like it, remember that you are strong! And look for opportunities to bear the weaknesses of others. Somebody you know needs help with a heavy load.

WE ARE
Filled with God's Goodness

> **Romans 15:14** You also are full of goodness, filled with all knowledge, and able to instruct one another.

My dad pastored small churches throughout North Carolina for fifty-five years. And frequently, when I encounter people who knew him, they will often remark, "Your dad was a good man."

Yes, there's still something to be said for a little old-fashioned goodness. We should never forget that it is listed as one aspect of the fruit of the Spirit (Gal. 5:22). When the Holy Spirit inhabits our lives, he will produce goodness through us.

This resounding affirmation that we are "full of goodness" is found at the very beginning of Paul's concluding words to the believers in Rome. He was aware that he had written to them "boldly" on several points throughout his letter (v. 15), using strong warnings to remind them of things they already knew. He wanted to assure these early Christians, however, that he had confidence they could live godly lives.

As Paul said, "goodness" when teamed with "knowledge" enables us to "instruct" or admonish one another. This phrase — "filled with all knowledge" — is not to be taken in an absolute sense, as if the Roman believers had nothing else to learn. If this were the case, Paul's letter to them would have been an unnecessary redundancy. (Remember, this is the same author who declared in 1 Corinthians 13:9 that we only "know in part" for the time being.) He meant, however, that they had a solid, well-rounded understanding of what it meant to be a Christian.

So one of our goals in seeking knowledge from God is that he may fill us with all goodness. That's because goodness and knowledge are absolutely essential if we are to admonish one another.

If we attempt to admonish without goodness, our words may have the effect of cruel criticism. If we attempt to admonish without biblically informed truth, our words will have only the impact of opinion. But if we admonish with biblical truth out of a heart of goodness, we will speak words of healing that encourage and lift up.

WE ARE
Not Spiritually Lacking

> **1 Corinthians 1:7** You do not lack any spiritual gift as you eagerly wait for the revelation of our Lord Jesus Christ.

I remember as a child dragging a few pennies and nickels out of my pocket, hoping to purchase a desired object, only to discover that I was lacking in resources. We've all had this experience in one form or another—some occasions being much more embarrassing or dangerous than others. To be lacking can sometimes lead a person to despair.

Paul told the Corinthian believers, however, that they were not lacking in any gift. This "gift" could be (1) the gift of salvation, (2) God's good gifts in general, or (3) his special gifts for ministry, otherwise known as spiritual gifts which enable us to serve him. The reference to "all speaking and all knowledge" in verse 5 suggests that Paul had in mind special gifts for ministry, but I would hasten to add that all of the above are implied by the broadness of his statement.

Our basis and assurance for embracing this promise is the grace of God, which we received "in Christ Jesus" the moment we believed (v. 4). Don't let anyone confuse you by suggesting that your salvation is not complete until you experience a second work of grace, a later infilling of the Spirit. God has held back nothing that would better enable you to live victoriously and to do his work through his church. Our problem is not a matter of *sufficiency* but one of *surrender.*

Let me say it one more time: you have all the gifts you need to please your heavenly Father. "He did not even spare His own Son, but offered Him up for us all; how will He not also with Him grant us everything?" (Rom. 8:32). It is staggering to contemplate what could be accomplished through our lives if we would begin living according to our potential.

How, then, do we move from potential to practice? 1) Commit to use your gifts in service to the Father, 2) ask him to reveal all that he has given to you, 3) begin to act on God's promises in your life, and 4) join other Christians in serving him.

WE ARE
in Christ Jesus

> **1 Corinthians 1:30** You are in Christ Jesus, who for us became wisdom from God.

This is one of the most frequently used images in the writings of the apostle Paul to describe the personal relationship that the believer has with Christ. But what does it mean to be "in Christ"?

It means that Christ is the very source of our lives. He is the atmosphere in which the believer lives. Not only does our source of *supply* come from God, our very *lives* come from him. In another context Paul says it this way: "For me, living is Christ" (Phil. 1:21).

Any picture or analogy will always fall short of expressing the truth, but perhaps a simple picture might help. We might speak of living "in" a house, or driving "in" a car. In each instance we're speaking about our location "inside" them and the consequent privileges we derive from them. When we live in a house, for example, we enjoy the benefits of its protection from stormy weather. We are kept warm by its heating system and made comfortable by its furnishings. When we're in a car, we enjoy the benefit of traveling faster and safer than we might travel on foot. We depend on its power to convey us to our destination. In other words, we enjoy the benefits of our position in the house or in the car.

So when the Bible speaks of being "in Christ," it too speaks of the believer's position and privilege. By virtue of our being in Christ, we experience certain blessings. In verse 30 alone, Paul speaks of four of these:

Wisdom —not eloquence or worldly philosophy, but the message of the cross.

Righteousness —acquittal for our sins, based on the blamelessness of Christ.

Sanctification —the state of being holy before God, becoming more like Christ.

Redemption —bought back from sin, our penalty paid.

I've got good news. You are "in Christ" by his doing. You can't earn it. You don't deserve it. But if you have trusted Christ as Savior, it is a reality. You are "in" Christ Jesus!

WE ARE
God's Field and Building

> **1 Corinthians 3:9** We are God's co-workers. You are God's field, God's building.

My dad loved his garden, which he would till in the spring with a stubborn old mule he borrowed from a neighbor. I often asked my dad why he struggled behind that old mule even though countless friends had volunteered the use of their tractors. He never gave me a satisfactory answer, but I am convinced that he simply liked walking in the freshly plowed soil and savoring the aroma of the earth. This was his field and he loved it. It was an extension of his creativity, the arena where he saw the potential for new life.

The word translated as "field" in this verse occurs only once in the New Testament. The Greek word behind it can refer either to the field itself or to the process of cultivation. In the same way, the word translated "building" can either signify the building proper or the process of erecting it.

These twin images of fields and buildings are from two different worlds, yet they reveal that we are both the *agricultural* and *architectural* work being done by God in the world today.

For example, he sows the good seed of the Word in our lives—tilling, weeding, and watering so that the seed might take root and produce much fruit. Some of these actions may seem painful for the moment, but his desire is to grow in us a bountiful harvest.

At the same time, he is also at work erecting our lives, building us into the kind of people that he can inhabit for his own purpose, polishing and finishing the rough edges and unsightly corners, making us brighter expressions of his grace and glory.

Often when we read the Bible and see the mighty acts of God recorded there, we wonder, "Where is God at work today?" This "we are" statement affirms, however, that God is at work *in and through us.* Just as my dad took joy and pride in his field, so our heavenly Father takes joy and pride in us, working in us so that he can manifest himself through us.

WE ARE
God's Temple

> **1 Corinthians 3:16** Don't you know that you are God's sanctuary and that the Spirit of God lives in you?

The word translated "sanctuary" or "temple" in this verse is singular, but the "you" is plural. So in this instance, Paul was not focusing on the fact—though true—that our individual bodies are the temple of the Spirit, as he later expressed in 1 Corinthians 6:19. Instead, he was focusing on the *church* as being the corporate community of believers through which God reveals himself in our world.

Does your local church function as the place where people encounter the very presence of God? Paul underlined this theme of *presence* by indicating that the "Spirit of God" dwells in us. The Spirit is the indwelling presence of God made manifest in his temple—his people. The creator of the universe wants to make his mighty presence known in the world today through us! What a sobering, exciting thought to imagine!

The church is such a critical issue to the Father, Paul said that if anyone destroyed the temple of God, God would destroy that person (v. 17). Someone who would tear down or work against the unity, witness, and integrity of God's people is guilty of a sin with great gravity, because God's temple is holy (v. 17)—dedicated to and set apart for his own purposes.

While no individual or group could ever destroy the church universal, it is definitely possible for someone's disunity and behavior to destroy a local church. The church is the bride of Christ, and the bridegroom is jealous for his bride, desiring to keep her holy. This is why our relationship to other believers is of vital concern to our Father. The gathering of his people is the place where his presence and power are made known today.

Do you have a healthy and productive relationship with a local church? Are you involved, using your gifts, talents, and time in such a way that God's presence is made known? Does your attitude contribute to its unity? Does your behavior protect its purity? We are the temple of God.

WE ARE
the Members of Christ

> **1 Corinthians 6:15** Do you not know that your bodies are the members of Christ?

I have had the pleasure of knowing numerous elderly couples who have shared a lifetime of marital togetherness. They became so identified as "one flesh" that people actually spoke of them in a singular fashion. I have also watched as death momentarily separated them. Even though they knew all the resurrection promises, their grief was deep because a part of their own being had been ripped asunder.

Christians are united to Christ in a similar relationship, to the point that our bodies are declared to be "members of Christ." This is why Paul bluntly asked the Corinthian believers, some of whom were obviously guilty of sexual misconduct, "Should I take the members of Christ and make them members of a prostitute?" (v. 15). The horrible thing about sin, particularly sexual sin, is that we "take" or "take away" (as some translations put it) the members of the body, thus rendering them ineffective for their proper use. This is a horrible profaning of our bodies, which have been redeemed at the exorbitant "price" of Christ's death (v. 20).

What then should be our response to this warning? We should make it our habitual practice to "flee from sexual immorality" (v. 18). The verb here is a present imperative, indicating a continual action. We must always monitor our thoughts and actions, ensuring that we are not guilty of "taking away" that which belongs to Christ. Our vigilance must include those things we watch, read, talk about, and treasure in our thoughts. We cannot defeat sexual temptation unless we actively "flee immorality," avoiding all the things that can tempt us to sexual misconduct.

"Your body is a sanctuary of the Holy Spirit" (v. 19). God's Holy Spirit actually dwells in you by virtue of God's gracious gift. We do not belong to ourselves; we belong to God. For this reason we should gladly and joyfully glorify God in our bodies, remembering that we indeed are "members of Christ."

WE ARE
Known by God

> **1 Corinthians 8:3** If anyone loves God, he is known by Him.

I have a picture in our den that shows President George W. Bush and me standing side by side. It is a treasured possession, but one that can be somewhat misleading. The picture was made several years ago when he was the governor of Texas and we were both attending (along with a horde of other well-wishers) a celebration honoring Dr. W. A. Criswell.

Occasionally, guests who see this picture in our home will ask if I know the President. Well, I have met him and I have spoken to him, but I don't really know him. Even more to the point, I am quite certain that he doesn't know *me*.

But being known by the President or another celebrity is one thing. Being known by God is quite another. Paul declared that those who love God are "known" by God. Man's love for God is always to be understood in the light of his love for us. "God's love was revealed among us in this way: God sent His One and Only Son into the world so that we might live through Him" (1 John 4:9). He proved His love for us "in that while we were still sinners Christ died for us" (Rom. 5:8). Thus it is clear that the person who loves God is one who has responded to God's love initiative.

This is not only a wonderful truth; it is a comforting reality. No matter what you face today, you can be assured he is intimately concerned about the details of your life. His knowledge of you assures you of his care for you.

Is there something you are facing that no one else knows about? Do you have private fears and doubts that you have been afraid to share with anyone else? Do you have deep hidden scars that are not visible to those closest to you? They are all known by God. So you can trust him with your inner thoughts and struggles. He loves you so much that he gave his Son to die for you . . . so that you could be "known by Him."

WE ARE
the Aroma of Christ

> **2 Corinthians 2:15** We are
> the fragrance of Christ among
> those who are being saved.

Among my fondest memories of childhood are the regular visits we made to my Grandma Kincaid's house. As we crossed the wooden bridge over the creek, her white frame house loomed larger than life—perched on the hillside, surrounded by fields of corn, secluded in the midst of several hundred acres of North Carolina mountain land. All of my memories about these visits are pleasant ones.

But the lingering sensation is one of *smell*. My grandmother cooked on a wood stove, and the smells that emanated from her kitchen were beyond description. The aroma of burning wood, mingled with the steam seeping from pots on the stove, were childhood fragrances I will never forget.

The Old Testament sacrifices were frequently described in terms of their fragrance. When Noah left the ark, he built an altar and sacrificed a burnt offering. And "the Lord smelled the pleasing aroma" (Gen. 8:21). We, too, are now a "living sacrifice" to God—"holy and pleasing to God" (Rom. 12:1). He is delighted by the sweet aroma of our service to him. Not only that, we spread "the scent of knowing Him" to those around us "in every place" we go (v. 14) as we witness for Christ through our actions and words. This is not an option for the believer. We are commanded to do this.

This aroma has such an impact that it becomes the fragrance of "life" to those who are being saved, like the indescribably sweet smell of a washed and powdered newborn. When we share the gospel, it always has the potential of manifesting the smell of new life among those we're around.

Not everyone, however, will respond to our message of hope and rebirth. Thus, to those who reject the gospel, this combination of the truth and our presence becomes "the stench of death." They cannot get past the scent of their own condemnation long enough to embrace and enjoy Christ's resurrection life. Are you spreading his fragrance through your behavior and your witness?

WE ARE
Given Over to Death

> **2 Corinthians 4:11** We who
> live are always given over to
> death because of Jesus.

Before you make up your mind not to claim this "we are" promise, I encourage you to look at the intended outcome. We are given over to death "so that Jesus' life may also be revealed in our mortal flesh."

Paul faced many afflictions and persecutions throughout his life and ministry, yet these ordeals did not cause him to despair. He had to be ready to suffer physically and mentally, willing to be misunderstood and hated for the sake of the gospel. He was never sure he would live through the day. Yet his suffering did not overwhelm him or make him bitter because he had absolute confidence that all these challenges served only to reveal the life of Jesus through his "mortal flesh."

True, the life of Jesus will not be fully manifested in our bodies until the future resurrection, when our physical bodies will be transformed into spiritual ones. But this process has already started! And any event of suffering or hardship serves only to reveal the treasure hidden in the "clay jars" or "earthly vessels" we call our bodies (v. 7). Jesus reveals his life and power through our suffering and weakness.

This passage came to have special meaning for our seminary community in Fort Worth when several of our students were martyred in the shootings at Wedgewood Baptist Church in September 1999. The media gave round-the-clock coverage to this event, expressing amazement at the victorious testimony they heard from those impacted by the shootings.

At a community-wide remembrance service, one person expressed it well when he thanked God "that he wastes nothing." In the world's eyes, the death of seven young people was *nothing but* a tremendous waste. Yet Christ's life was revealed out of this tragedy. His church again proved that we can be "struck down but not destroyed" (v. 9). You can be assured that the Lord can take every event in your life—even the most difficult—and reveal his life through you as you surrender yourself to him.

WE ARE
Protected from Fear of Death

> **2 Corinthians 5:8** We are confident and satisfied to be out of the body and at home with the Lord.

Death is not a subject we like to talk about. We avoid the topic, perhaps believing that if we refuse to discuss it, it will simply disappear like the shadows hiding under our childhood bed. To speak of death brings us face to face with our own mortality, taking us into areas that involve both mystery and faith.

In the early verses of chapter 5, Paul pictured death as the tearing down of an "earthly house." We have grown comfortable living in this earthly house—these bodies of ours—and thus we resist both its aging and its final destruction. Paul took courage, however, in the promise that believers have a dwelling in heaven we can one day "put on" like new clothing (v. 2).

Still, we struggle with this, because we are familiar with our earthly dwelling and not our heavenly one. Therefore, we wonder how this transition will be handled.

Yet we do have a pledge from God that gives us absolute confidence in the integrity of his promises: the presence of the Holy Spirit (v. 5). Anxiety and despair are inconsistent with the witness the Spirit bears in our hearts.

For this reason we can and should have courage, emboldened by the fact that the Lord is with us now through the ministry of the Holy Spirit, and that when we leave this present body we will be visibly in the Lord's presence (v. 6). The living reality of the Spirit and the absolute reliability of God's promises should enable us to walk by faith (v. 7).

One of the things I like best about this promise is that it has both present and future consequences. As Paul wrote in verse 9, "Whether we are at home or away, we make it our aim to be pleasing to Him." The presence of the Holy Spirit gives us unshakable confidence as we face the future, enabling us to behave in a manner that is pleasing to the Lord in our present body. God our Father has banished the frightening shadows of death from us. Now we can really live.

WE ARE
a New Creation

> **2 Corinthians 5:17** If anyone is in Christ, there is a new creation; old things have passed away, and look, new things have come.

I have had Christians say to me that they knew for certain they had been born again, but they didn't see any evidence that they were a "new creation." They still struggled with some of the same habits and behavior patterns that were part of their lifestyle before they became Christians. They wanted to know why a new creation person still had traits of his old creation.

Well, when we receive Christ, we do become a new being. The act of new creation has already taken place in the death and resurrection of Jesus Christ. And because we are "in Christ" (1 Cor. 1:30), all the benefits of the new creation have become our family heritage. But the process of becoming all we are born to be remains an ongoing work of the Holy Spirit. Receiving Christ does not mean that all our old habits and memories are instantly destroyed.

This tension between what has already occurred (new creation) and what is in process (our transformation into the image of our Father) dictates that we live by faith. Think about it! We still live in a physical world that does not appear to be radically changed, and we still manifest traces of our former sinful behavior. Thus we must live in the midst of the *old* creation in terms of our *new* creation. And that requires faith in order to navigate!

In practical terms this means you must take your Father at his word. Have you struggled to believe some of the wonderful "we are" passages we have been studying together? Yet they are true — *simply because God declares them to be so!* Therefore, you need to begin living in the light of these promises of God. Claim them by faith and begin to act upon these accomplished facts.

This might be a good time to look back through the earlier promises of this book and ask yourself, "Am I living based on God's promises?" Memorize these promises, repeat them regularly to yourself, and ask the Spirit to reveal in you his act of new creation.

WE ARE
Ambassadors for Christ

> **2 Corinthians 5:20** We are ambassadors for Christ; certain that God is appealing through us, we plead on Christ's behalf.

In my pre-teen years, I belonged to an organization called Royal Ambassadors—in part because my preacher dad was our RA director (who didn't give me much choice in the matter) and also because I looked forward to the football games we played before the chapter meetings. But a few of the things I learned as we studied God's Word and talked about missions did stick with me. One of them was this statement: "An ambassador is one who represents the person of the king at the court of another."

Just as a political ambassador is entrusted with a nation's terms of peace, ambassadors of Christ have been given the "message of reconciliation" (v. 19). This message is at once profound and simple: "In Christ, God was reconciling the world to Himself, not counting their trespasses against them." The only qualification to be an ambassador of Christ is that we must first have experienced the reconciliation we are now declaring (v. 18).

This title of ambassador is one that should make us both proud and humble. We represent the King of kings! As his representative we do not speak in our own name, labor under our own authority, nor communicate our own message. We speak with the authority of Christ himself, expressing the message we have been commanded to declare. As Paul said, it is as though "God is appealing through us" (v. 20).

Who do you know that needs to be reconciled to God? Have you explained to them the terms of the peace treaty, how "He made the One who did not know sin to be sin for us, so that we might become the righteousness of God in Him"? (v. 21). Have you pleaded with them to be reconciled to God?

The resurrected Christ who exercises all authority has commissioned us to go into all the world and make disciples in his name. And he will go with us! "We are" certain of that!

WE ARE
Strong When We Are Weak

> **2 Corinthians 12:10**
> Because of Christ, I am pleased
> in weaknesses. . . . For when I
> am weak, then I am strong.

I find the Bible to be so refreshing and challenging to my traditional way of thinking. Earthly reckoning and heavenly reckoning are often diametrically opposed. You know what I mean: The first shall be last and the last shall be first. The greatest among you will be the least. If you want to lead, you must first stoop and serve. And here's another one to add to your list: when we are weak, then we are strong.

Some of Paul's opponents in Corinth boasted in their visions and spectacular spiritual abilities. They then questioned *Paul's* ability, pointing up the contrast and suggesting that "his physical presence is weak, and his public speaking is despicable" (2 Cor. 10:10). Pretty cutting criticism for a preacher to bear!

But Paul was reluctant to play their game. Not only did he resist boasting in his own credentials, he turned the tables on his opponents and boasted about his hardship and suffering (2 Cor. 11:24–28). Even when he admitted to having a visionary experience more spectacular than anything his accusers could claim to have witnessed, Paul still refused to "boast" about anything other than his "weaknesses" (v. 5). That's when he made this wonderful discovery — "When I am weak, then I am strong."

We all need to be reminded that the Christian life is not just *difficult*; it is *impossible!* Yes, it is impossible to live the Christian life in human strength, although we are all prone to try doing so. Such a strategy will always result in both pride and discouragement — *pride* from the false presumption that we can do it on our own, and *discouragement* from the stark reality that we can do nothing apart from Christ.

Have you made the wonderful discovery that when you admit the weakness of your human flesh you will experience the abundance of his strength? In what area of life do you most need to know his strength? Are you willing to accept and even rejoice in your weakness so that you might live according to his strength?

WE ARE
Crucified with Christ

> **Galatians 2:19–20** I have been crucified with Christ; and I no longer live, but Christ lives in me.

Crucifixion was one of the cruelest forms of capital punishment in the first century. Death came slowly and painfully from the awful combination of blood loss, physical exhaustion, and strangulation that occurred as the lungs filled with fluid. But for Paul, his crucifixion with Christ was a moment to be celebrated. A devout and rigorous Jew, Paul had attempted to appease God by living up to the perfect standards of the law. Yet he had discovered what every person both before and since has learned: no one can live without breaking God's law.

Therefore, Paul found himself a condemned criminal before God. His only hope came through the death of Jesus Christ, who had lived a perfect life and accepted the punishment for man's sinfulness. So Paul turned to Christ, identifying with him in his death.

In the New Testament community, this fact was most clearly illustrated through baptism. "Are you unaware," Paul once wrote, "that all of us who were baptized into Christ Jesus were baptized into His death?" (Rom. 6:3). When the new believer is plunged beneath the water, it symbolizes his death to self. When he is brought up again, it depicts his new life with Christ to be lived in the Spirit.

When I was pastor in Norfolk, Virginia, I was privileged to know a number of military chaplains, several of whom were deployed with our troops in Iraq. One of them explained how they had created a makeshift baptismal for the soldiers who had professed faith in Christ. They had lined a wooden coffin with a plastic body bag and then filled it with water. The coffin, originally built to hold the remains of soldiers killed in combat, had been commandeered for a much higher purpose.

I was moved by the graphic picture this baptismal coffin brought to mind — "buried with Him by baptism into death . . . so we too may walk in a new way of life" (Rom. 6:4). I think Paul would have liked that.

WE ARE
Heirs with Christ

> **Galatians 3:29** If you are Christ's, then you are Abraham's seed, heirs according to the promise.

Somewhere in the recesses of my childhood memory is the faint recollection of a television program that sought to find missing heirs. They located people who had obtained an inheritance through the death of a family member or friend but were totally unaware of its existence.

Some of the stories, as you might imagine, made for good television viewing, like when a poor couple who had lived on sparse resources would discover that they had inherited substantial wealth. A few stories, however, were quite sad. Some of the missing heirs had lived a lifetime in virtual poverty, only to discover in the final years of their lives that they had long been entitled to a vast sum of money.

Did you know that as a Christian you are an heir of God? Do you know about your inheritance? Are you taking advantage of all that is available to you in Christ?

In Galatians 3:28–29 we find two "we are" statements. First, we are all "one in Christ Jesus." Therefore, the traditional distinctions that divide people—cultural, linguistic, religious, and gender—are rendered insignificant as far as access to the Father is concerned. (This does not suggest that earthly role distinctions like man and woman are rendered unnecessary by our salvation. It simply means that neither superiority nor inferiority have any place in the new society of believers.) It is wonderful to know that earthly restrictions cannot impede our access to God.

Secondly, "in Christ" we are all recipients of the one inheritance made available through him. We have all become members of God's family, and our sonship qualifies us to be heirs of the promise (v. 29). We now share in the Father's nature. The Holy Spirit indwells us to produce his character in us as we surrender to him daily.

As believers in Christ, we are not destined to live in spiritual poverty, like missing heirs who are unaware of the vast resources made available to us through our inheritance.

WE ARE
Sons, Not Slaves

> **Galatians 4:7** You are no longer a slave, but a son; and if a son, then an heir through God.

I grew up in the small town of Thomasville, North Carolina. Most of my friends were from families with moderate incomes. And although there were a few families with significant wealth who could afford to live a little "higher on the hog," the distinctions weren't all that great.

One day, however, our junior high was awed by the news that one of our classmates had suddenly become a millionaire. Apparently, a grandparent had died and left a sizeable estate to her. As you might imagine, her popularity soared. Young men who had not previously thought of her in romantic terms quickly became infatuated.

Quickly, however, the interest dissipated when she explained that she did not have access to the funds until she turned twenty-one. Even though she had indeed inherited great wealth, this windfall was to be controlled by her guardian until the specified date. To our youthful minds, being an heir without access to the inheritance was like slavery.

In Christ, however, we already have access to our inheritance. We are "no longer" slaves but sons. My good friend, Maxie Dunnam, writing in *The Communicator's Commentary*, challenged me to look at the changes "sonship" makes in our everyday living. Let me paraphrase and add to his thoughts:

First, sonship changes our identity and self-worth. To know we are loved and accepted by the Father transforms our understanding of who we are. *Second, it changes our praying.* We are not groveling before a distant despot who doesn't understand or care about our needs. We sit in the lap of a loving Father who knows what we need even before we ask. *Third, it changes our understanding about the source of our strength.* We have inherited the resources of the Father; thus we can do all things through him who strengthens us. *Fourth, it changes our desire for ministry.* We now serve the Father with the joy of a son given the privilege of joining him in his activity.

WE ARE
Not under the Law

> **Galatians 5:18** If you are led by the Spirit, you are not under the law.

Have you ever tried to overcome a habit by the force of sheer willpower? You know firsthand, then, the pain of the struggle and the disappointment that comes with repeated setbacks.

Knowing this, it is little wonder that the marketplace has produced countless aids to assist us in our battles against compulsive behaviors. They've created patches to help an individual quit smoking, pills to help us avoid overeating, fingernail polish that tastes so bad you will never want to munch on your nails again, and filters for your computer or television that keep you from viewing objectionable material.

Yes, we all know that the flesh is weak, and we all struggle to overcome our bad habits. But when we are being led by the Spirit, we are no longer defenseless against the flesh. We are not left alone with the advice to "just try harder" or "just stop doing that." The Spirit of God enables us to defeat the flesh.

This is because when we receive Jesus Christ as our personal Savior, we are no longer under the law. Is that because the law is bad? No, God's law is good, reflecting his character. It was given for man's protection. But according to Galatians 3:24, the law was merely our tutor or "guardian," designed to lead us to Christ. Now that we have received the One who "redeemed us from the curse of the law by becoming a curse for us" (Gal. 3:13), the Holy Spirit has taken up residence in our lives. We are free to obey, not doomed to our own failure.

Wouldn't you like to produce the fruit of the Spirit on a regular basis? You can! Those who belong to Jesus Christ have crucified the flesh with its passions and desires (v. 24). We must now begin to walk by the Spirit. So if you are certain that you are born again yet are not experiencing led-by-the-Spirit victory, confess your sin and ask him to fill your life, to produce his fruit in you through his powerful presence.

WE ARE
Sealed with the Holy Spirit

> **Ephesians 1:13** You also, when you heard the word of truth . . . were sealed with the promised Holy Spirit.

When it came time to buy our first house, the excitement and anticipation created a sweaty palm condition. I can still remember writing the check for the down payment, then signing the contract that promised we would make future payments until the entire obligation was met. Finally, a notary pressed the document with a seal and the transaction was finalized. Without the application of the seal, all our promises and agreements were just words on paper.

Paul used a similar image—the seal—to talk about the ministry of the Holy Spirit, who seals us in Christ and guarantees our ultimate, full redemption. This process has at least three results:

• *Authentication*. Perhaps you have seen a family crest on a signet ring, which can be pressed into melted wax to seal a letter or document. This seal gives assurance that the document is authentic.

• *Ownership*. The family seal also confirms a rightful claim to the property being bought. The document in question cannot be ascribed to another's hand.

• *Protection*. If you received a document that was sealed, you could tell that it had not been tampered with. It would bear the proof of being secure.

When you receive Christ, the Father seals you with his family crest by filling you with the Holy Spirit, identifying you as an authentic believer and ascribing to you all the promises of salvation. Through him you have access to "every spiritual blessing in the heavens, in Christ" (v. 3)—sonship, redemption, forgiveness, holiness, and more. Above this you have been sealed for all eternity, guaranteed his full and final protection against death and loss.

The Holy Spirit, then, is like the down payment on your salvation—the assurance that your future is secure, that your hope in Christ is fixed. Because you possess the Holy Spirit as a seal on your heart, your whole life is given the freedom to be a benediction, an offering of worship to God, "to the praise of His glory" (v. 14).

WE ARE
Created to Do Good

> **Ephesians 2:10** We are His
> creation — created in Christ
> Jesus for good works.

I love to walk through craft bazaars
and am always astounded by the creativity
some people possess, how they can work
with nearly every conceivable substance to
fashion pieces of art and beauty — everything from sock puppets and corn shuck
dolls to ceramics and priceless jewelry.

I myself enjoy working with watercol-
ors. I am not very proficient and therefore
will never be known as an artist, but I do
derive great satisfaction from the paintings
I create. They are a part of me. They reflect
my personality and my interests. Even as
children, we love to show our parents and
friends what we have created.

Did you know God views you as his
workmanship? Man was created in God's
image to enjoy eternal fellowship with him.
Yet the sad story of man's rebellion and sin
entered God's perfect creation, and we all
alike participated in the fallout.

Ephesians 2 picks up the story in the middle of this tragic account, reminding us of the hope God injected into our hopeless situation. Out of the abundance of his love, he "made us alive" again in him (vv. 4–5), not through any good works of our own but simply as "God's gift" to us (v. 8). Paul summarized this redemptive act by writing this wonderful "we are" acclamation: "We are His creation."

When one of my watercolor paintings is defaced, I can do nothing to restore it to its original beauty. God, however, has restored us through his redemptive work — but not so we can sit on a shelf and gather dust. We have been recreated with intentionality. We are not saved *by* our good works; we are saved *for* good works "which God prepared ahead of time so that we should walk in them." We are designed by him so that good works flow from us without conscious effort. These are the fruit and evidence of his Spirit who indwells us. God's original plan for you has been restored through redemption, and he has a wonderful plan for your life because you are his workmanship.

WE ARE
Fellow Citizens with the Saints

> **Ephesians 2:19** You are no longer foreigners and strangers, but fellow citizens with the saints.

The first Christians were Jews who dared to believe that Jesus was the promised Messiah. Soon, however, the early church faced a dilemma when Gentiles began responding to the preaching of the gospel. *Should the Gentiles*, they asked, *be accepted as full members of the church?*

Paul issued a reminder in Ephesians 2, showing how excluded the Gentiles had been throughout history. Verse 12 reads: "At that time you were without the Messiah, excluded from the citizenship of Israel, and foreigners to the covenants of the promise, with no hope and without God in the world." This shows the distance that existed between Jews and Gentiles in Paul's day—and which sadly echoes the feeling of many persons in our world today.

But the tearing down of the barrier that divided Jew and Gentile was accomplished through the blood of Christ (v. 13).

Christ reconciled these two groups, making them "one new man" through his own death on the cross (vv. 15–16), providing both of them with access "by one Spirit to the Father" (v. 18). This great theological truth establishes the foundation for the declaration: "You are fellow citizens with the saints." We are no longer strangers to one another. In Christ, national restrictions have been removed and Gentiles enjoy the same privileges as Jews.

Perhaps you may be wondering how all this talk about Jews and Gentiles relates to us today. When we received Christ, we not only became his workmanship individually (2:10) but were also born into his family. We received new citizenship papers. We now belong to a community of faith with roots extending all the way back to God's eternal purposes for his church. We take our seat alongside Abraham, Jacob, Isaac, Paul, and Timothy. So in order for us to experience spiritual growth, we must find fellowship with our "fellow saints." We must be part of a church who believes and teaches God's Word. He wants to build us together into his dwelling place on earth.

WE ARE
Christ's Household

> **Hebrews 3:6** Christ was faithful as a Son over His household, whose household we are.

I had the wonderful good fortune of growing up in a loving household. My dad, a Baptist pastor for fifty-five years, modeled God's love for me. I loved being around him, whether it was at a football game, on a camping trip, or at a church meeting. My mom was the consummate mother. She kept the house clean, cooked wonderful meals, and kept us all organized. Even my older brother and sister were a joy to me (although I would never have told them at the time). They were my heroes as I was growing up. All of my memories are of a happy childhood.

I was privileged to marry into another wonderful family, the Moores. My wife and our children took vacations with our extended family, spent holidays together, and developed "household" relationships that continue to this day. There is nothing quite like family.

The original audience for the book of Hebrews knew what it was like to be disinherited by their earthly families. Faith in Christ for those living in a first-century context often came with real persecution, including the severed ties of lifelong family relationships. This is why the statement that believers were members of Christ's "household" brought such great encouragement to those who had been shunned and rejected by parents and relatives.

You may not personally face these same challenges. Physical persecution may be infrequent in America, and ostracism by one's family does not usually accompany conversion. But for some, faith in Christ does come at the cost of family togetherness. If this has happened to you, take courage in the fact that you are a welcome member at the table in Christ's household.

All of us, actually—in one form or another—face consequences as a result of our faith. Biblical convictions can lead us to make unpopular decisions and be misunderstood. But our place in Christ's family can give us the confidence and boldness to stand.

WE ARE
Not Quitters

{ **Hebrews 10:39** We are not those who draw back and are destroyed, but those who have faith and obtain life. }

If you are a sports fan, you understand the nature of athletic events. You don't mind seeing a team honestly beaten if they did their best until the final whistle. But if you've watched many sporting events at all, you've seen what happens when a team gives up, becoming so defeated in their own minds that they quit before the time expires.

The writer of Hebrews was concerned that some of the early believers might be tempted to quit or "draw back" before the race was over. He wanted them to understand that they were winners, that they had the resources to endure.

Few of us can imagine experiencing intense hostility for believing in Christ, but such was the case for the early believers, many of whom were put to death for their faith. This is why the inspired writer of Hebrews quoted an Old Testament passage in verse 38 to remind them: "My righteous one will live by faith." Faith (he was telling them) is not only *saving* faith, but it is that which sustains us and gives substance to our hope. Our faith, sufficient to raise us from the depths of our sin condition, can also sustain us as we face various trials.

God works through our circumstances to complete our faith. Because we know he is altogether good and powerful, we can be patient in the process and confident in his character. We know that he can and will work everything to our advantage. So we are able to remain loyal. We are not those who "draw back."

What have you faced recently that made you wonder if you could stand firm? Are you dealing with circumstances that make you want to throw in the towel? Are there mornings when the thought of getting out of bed requires all the inner resources you have? Are there people at school or at work who harass you because of your stand for Christ? Take comfort, then, from this promise: "We are not those who draw back." The sovereign God of the universe is working for you in all these things.

WE ARE
Protected by God's Power

> **1 Peter 1:5** [You] are being protected by God's power for a salvation that is ready to be revealed in the last time.

"Life has been forever changed since September 11!" How many times have you heard that phrase repeated? It is true that our lives have been radically altered in certain respects. We are all more acutely aware that life is both precious and fragile.

It comes as no surprise, then, that many of the industries which specialize in items designed for personal protection are doing well. Home security systems, mace, firearms, and the like have experienced robust sales. Yet we know it's impossible to provide absolute protection when a zealot will fly a plane full of innocent people into the side of a building, or when a sniper randomly shoots unsuspecting victims. We can't go to work wearing full body armor, and not all of us can quit flying on airplanes. But there is a promise of protection that goes beyond all earthly possibilities. We are "protected by God's power."

Peter addressed his letter to early Christians who were dealing face-to-face with personal danger. Yet as Peter said to them, they were also chosen by God (v. 2) and were the recipients of an "inheritance that is imperishable, uncorrupted, and unfading, kept in heaven for you" (v. 4).

All of us understand the term *inheritance*. We don't deserve an inheritance, nor do we do anything to obtain it. It usually comes to us because of family connections. Still, it is an earthly inheritance, capable of being lost, stolen, spent, or destroyed.

As believers, however, our inheritance was purchased by the death of Jesus. It is actually being reserved in heaven for us, inscribed with our names and "ready to be revealed in the last time." And just as our inheritance is under the safe keeping of almighty God, so we—the heirs—are continually being kept pure and eternally safe by his power. We committed our life to him through faith, and through faith we experience his protection and provision.

What are you experiencing that causes you to fear? Have you brought it under the umbrella of God's protection?

WE ARE
God's People

> **1 Peter 2:10** Once you were not a people, but now you are God's people.

In 1 Peter 2:9–10, the apostle made five declarations about believers, culminating in this great affirmation: "You are God's people," meaning we are indeed royalty.

• *We are a chosen race.* The Jews had been chosen to experience God's blessing so that they might in turn be a blessing to the nations. But Peter announced that God had chosen a new people to be his chosen race through spiritual birth, not physical descent. All who receive Christ are members of God's chosen race.

• *We are a royal priesthood.* Not only have we been adopted by King Jesus and given the privilege of ruling with him, we have also been assigned to serve as God's ministers to mankind. In the phrase "royal priesthood," the ideas of ruling and serving are bound inextricably together. We rule with Jesus while ministering God's grace to all people.

• *We are a holy nation*. Most nations are marked by geographical boundaries and racial similarities, but our uniqueness as God's people is that we are marked by holiness. We bear the mark of our monarch, and we are holy as he is holy.

• *We are a people for his own possession*. God's people are formed by him in such a way that we show forth his character, grace, and magnificence. We are called to represent the One who has redeemed us and chosen us for his own, to display the virtues of him "who called [us] out of darkness into His marvelous light."

• *We are the people of God*. Peter wanted to remind his readers of their former estate, that they were once "not a people." Before we received mercy, we stood under the sentence of condemnation. But now we are the people of God, not because of any human merit but because of divine grace.

Have you discovered fellowship with other members of the royal priesthood and holy nation? Have you contemplated the vast privileges and responsibilities of your new citizenship? We are not just any old people. We are the people of God!

WE ARE
Blessed When We Are Cursed

> **1 Peter 4:14** If you are ridiculed for the name of Christ, you are blessed, because the Spirit of glory and of God rests on you.

We like the idea of being blessed. We sometimes speak of being blessed by a sermon or through Christian music. But how many of us want to access our blessing through the avenues of insult and ridicule?

Peter warned his readers that they should not be "surprised" whenever they went through persecution, "as if something unusual is happening to you" (v. 12). This is why we shouldn't be shocked when someone sues to have the words "under God" removed from the pledge to the flag, or when we are restricted from praying in Jesus' name in public settings. Instead, Peter said we should "rejoice," counting it a privilege to "share in the sufferings of the Messiah" (v. 13—which, by the way, are likely to get much worse in the days ahead.

But is this merely a *future* promise of blessing, a confirmation that we will have reason for rejoicing someday "at the revelation of His glory"? (v. 13). The point of verse 14 is to teach us that when we are reviled because we are standing for the name of Christ, we will be blessed even now by an unusual presence of the Holy Spirit to strengthen us.

Whenever I read this passage, it calls to mind the stoning of Stephen. Even as he was being persecuted to the point of death, he was able to gaze into heaven and see "God's glory, with Jesus standing at the right hand of God" (Acts 7:55). He was even given the strength and grace to call out, "Lord, do not charge them with this sin!" (Acts 7:60).

We should never seek out persecution as a way to encourage our martyr complex. Nor do we want to bring suffering upon ourselves as a result of our poor behavior (v. 15). "But if anyone suffers as a Christian, he should not be ashamed, but should glorify God with that name" (v. 16). When we are willing and able to do that, the Bible promises we will discover a life of blessing. As Jesus said, "Blessed are those who are persecuted for righteousness, because the kingdom of heaven is theirs" (Matt. 5:10).

WE ARE
Called God's Children

> **1 John 3:1** Look at how great a love the Father has given us, that we should be called God's children. And we are!

I am the proud father of three grown daughters, who are the delight of my life. I derive incredible joy from sharing in their accomplishments, and I count it a privilege whenever they call on me to help or just to listen. Their phone calls make my day! I can hardly wait to hear from them.

If I take such delight in *my* children, I can only imagine the joy God's children bring to him! This is made especially intriguing when we consider the Greek construction in this verse from 1 John, where the words "Father" and "us" are placed in such a manner as to underline the black-and-white contrast between our unworthiness and God's great love.

Truly, he has lavished an incomprehensible love toward us, transforming us from people deserving to be held at a distance into children loved enough to be gathered close and accepted. We could paraphrase verse 1: "To us poor sinners, the Father has lavishly bestowed the priceless right to be his children." I find it beyond belief that I can call the sovereign God of the universe my Father.

There is more good news, though, about being children of God. Some day "we will be like Him" (v. 2). We will never be deified, of course, but we are even now being transformed into his image. When we were saved, God began working in our lives to conform us to the image of his Son. Thus our future manifestation into his likeness is based on our present process of purification (v. 3). We are children of God, and we shall be like our Father.

A few years ago I was preaching in my home state of North Carolina. At the end of the message, an elderly pastor sought me out to tell me that he had been a close friend of my father. He then paid me one of the finest compliments I have ever received: "While listening to you tonight," he said, "I was reminded of your father. Your voice and your message put me in mind of him." How good to be called the children of God!

WE ARE
from God

One of my fondest memories from
high school was Friday night football. I
can remember those crisp, fall evenings as
if they were yesterday. Some of our opponents from much larger schools would
arrive in an impressive caravan of buses
carrying players, cheerleaders, band, and
boosters. But our coach would assemble
our small team in the dressing room and
give us a spirited pep talk, assuring us that
we were winners. He would challenge us
to embody the tradition of the Thomasville
Bulldogs.

John's readers were facing serious
challenges. False teachers were creating
confusion among the early church, seeking
to persuade, deceive, and dominate those
who put their hope in Christ. But victory
in this battle was not based on physical
strength and winning arguments; it was
based on the presence and power of God.

So in verses 4 and 6 of this chapter, John affirmed his readers with this "we are" statement: "We are from God." Our ability to stand as Christians against false teachers is based on our spiritual dependence upon the Father.

As the victorious line from verse 4 confirms, "The One who is in you is greater than the one who is in the world." We don't stand in our own strength. The victory has been won, and the Victor dwells in us. This is why John could assure his readers that they already possessed everything they needed to overcome the false prophets. The Holy Spirit would enable them to discern spiritual truth and not be deceived by false teachers.

Do not miss out on the power of this simply stated promise. Develop a consistent pattern of personal and corporate Bible study, at home and through your church, so you will know the Word. Seek out teachers who have a high view of the Scriptures, who teach the great doctrines of Christian truth as non-negotiable and worthy of defense. "We are from God," and we can never be defeated.

WE ARE
As He Is

{ **1 John 4:17** Love is perfected with us so that we may have confidence in the day of judgment; for we are as He is in this world. }

We have had a wonderful journey together, thinking about a few of the exciting "we are" faith statements in the Scripture. We finish with one containing a promise on how to have confidence concerning the "day of judgment." This concept of *judgment* makes most of us a bit uncomfortable. It reminds us of the specter of final exams. Our professors used to assure us that we should look forward to exams because they gave us a chance to demonstrate what we had learned. (We were concerned, however, that they might reveal something else!)

John wrote to tell us that our assurance in the face of judgment is fortified by the truth of who God is and what he has done in us—"for we are as He is in this world." This promise is based on God's "perfect love," which he manifested toward us in redemption and continues to express through our relationship with him as Father and child. In doing so, God produces his character in us by the indwelling Holy Spirit. And as we become more like him in this life, the evidence of his presence in us gives us confidence that he remains active in our lives and will not forsake us in judgment.

Jesus underlined this truth when he celebrated the Passover meal with his disciples: "Just as I have loved you, you must also love one another. By this all people will know that you are My disciples, if you have love for one another" (John 13:34–35).

Do you have confidence in the "day of judgment"? Have you accepted Christ as Savior? If you are not certain, I hope you will read through the gospel presentation found in the appendix. If you *are* certain you have been born again, yet you still have worries about judgment, perhaps you just need to ask the Father to perfect his love in you. For I assure you, as you grow in your ability to express his love, you will become increasingly more confident about the final exam.

APPENDIX

The promises of this book are based on one's relationship to Christ. If you have not yet entered a personal relationship with Jesus Christ, I encourage you to make this wonderful discovery today. I like to use the very simple acrostic—LIFE—to explain this, knowing that God wants you not only to inherit *eternal* life but also to experience *earthly* life to its fullest.

L = LOVE

It all begins with God's love. God created you in his image. This means you were created to live in relationship with him. *"For God loved the world in this way: He gave His One and Only Son, so that everyone who believes in Him will not perish but have eternal life" (John 3:16)*

But if God loves you and desires relationship with you, why do you feel so isolated from him?

I = ISOLATION

This isolation is created by our sin—our rebellion against God—which separates us from him and from others. *"For all have sinned and fall short of the glory of God"* (Rom. 3:23). *"For the wages of sin is death, but the gift of God is eternal life in Christ Jesus our Lord"* (Rom. 6:23).

You might wonder how you can overcome this isolation and have an intimate relationship with God.

F = FORGIVENESS

The only solution to man's isolation and separation from a holy God is forgiveness. *"For Christ also suffered for sins once for all, the righteous for the unrighteous, that he might bring you to God, after being put to death in the fleshly realm but made alive in the spiritual realm"* (1 Peter 3:18).

The only way our relationship can be restored with God is through the forgiveness of our sins. Jesus Christ died on the cross for this very purpose.

E = Eternal Life

You can have full and abundant life in this present life . . . and eternal life when you die. *"But to all who did receive Him, He gave them the right to be children of God, to those who believe in His name"* (John 1:12). *"A thief comes only to steal and to kill and to destroy. I have come that they may have life and have it in abundance"* (John 10:10).

Is there any reason you wouldn't like to have a personal relationship with God?

The Plan of Salvation

It's as simple as ABC. All you have to do is:

A = Admit you are a sinner. Turn from your sin and turn to God. *"Repent and turn back, that your sins may be wiped out so that seasons of refreshing may come from the presence of the Lord"* (Acts 3:19).

B = Believe that Jesus died for your sins and rose from the dead enabling you to have life. *"I have written these things to you who believe in the name of the Son of God, so that you may know that you have eternal life"* (1 John 5:13).

C = Confess verbally and publicly your belief in Jesus Christ. *"If you confess with your mouth, 'Jesus is Lord,' and believe in your heart that God raised Him from the dead, you will be saved. With the heart one believes, resulting in righteousness, and with the mouth one confesses, resulting in salvation"* (Rom. 10:9–10).

You can invite Jesus Christ to come into your life right now. Pray something like this:

"God, I admit that I am a sinner. I believe that you sent Jesus, who died on the cross and rose from the dead, paying the penalty for my sins. I am asking that you forgive me of my sin, and I receive your gift of eternal life. It is in Jesus' name that I ask for this gift. Amen."

Signed _____

Date _____

If you have a friend or family member who is a Christian, tell them about your decision. Then find a church that teaches the Bible, and let them help you go deeper with Christ.

Kingdom Promises

If you've enjoyed this book of Kingdom Promises, you may want to consider reading one of the others in the series:

We Are
0-8054-2781-3

We Can
0-8054-2780-5

But God
0-8054-2782-1

He Is
0-8054-2783-X

Available in stores nationwide and through major online retailers. For a complete look at Ken Hemphill titles, make sure to visit www.BHPublishingGroup.com/hemphill.